Country

Simon Stephens

Methuen Drama

Published by Methuen Drama

3 5 7 9 10 8 6 4 2

First published in 2004 by
Methuen Publishing Limited

Methuen Drama
A&C Black Ltd
36 Soho Square
London W1D 3QY

www.methuendrama.com

A CIP catalogue record for this book is available from the British Library

ISBN: 978-0-413-77468-2

Typeset by Country Setting, Kingsdown, Kent

ROYAL COURT   atc

The Royal Court Theatre and ATC present

COUNTRY MUSIC

by **Simon Stephens**

First performance at the Royal Court Jerwood Theatre Upstairs
Sloane Square, London on 24 June 2004.

Supported by Jerwood New Playwrights
JERWOOD
NEW PLAYWRIGHTS

COUNTRY MUSIC

by **Simon Stephens**

Cast
Jamie Carris **Lee Ross**
Matty Carris **Calum Callaghan**
Emma Carris **Laura Elphinstone**
Lynsey Sergeant **Sally Hawkins**

Director **Gordon Anderson**
Designer **Soutra Gilmour**
Lighting Designer **Charles Balfour**
Composer **Julian Swales**
Assistant Director **Steve Marmion**
Casting **Lisa Makin**
Production Manager **Sue Bird**
Stage Managers **Kieran Dicker, Marius Ronning**
Costume Supervisor **Iona Kenrick**
Company Voice Work **Patsy Rodenburg**

THE COMPANY

Simon Stephens (writer)
For the Royal Court: Herons, Bluebird (Choice Festival 1998).
Other theatre includes: Christmas (Bush); One Minute (ATC); Port (Royal Exchange, Manchester).
Radio includes: Five Letters Home to Elizabeth, Digging.
Awards include: Pearson Award for Best Play 2001 (Port) Pearson Bursary at the Royal Exchange, Manchester, Arts Council Resident Dramatist at the Royal Court in 2000.
Simon is Writers Tutor at the Royal Court Young Writers Programme.

Gordon Anderson (director)
For the Royal Court: Bluebird.
Other theatre includes: One Minute, Out of Our Heads, Arabian Night, In the Solitude of Cotton Fields (ATC); Great Expectations (Old Vic, Bristol); The Threesome, The Reckless are Dying Out, The Grand Ceremonial (Lyric, Hammersmith); Rib Cage (Royal Exchange, Manchester); Outside on the Street (Gate).
Opera includes: Manon (ETO); Hansel & Gretel (Scottish Opera); The Mikado (Grange Park Opera); The Silver Lake (Broomhill Opera).
Comedy includes: Catherine Tate, The League of Gentlemen, Navelgazing, Susan & Janice, Conversations with my Agent and projects for the Channel 4 Sitcom Festival.
Television: The Catherine Tate Show.
Gordon is Artistic Director of ATC.

Charles Balfour (lighting designer)
Theatre includes: Bash (Glasgow Citizens); Cake & Grace (Jade TC/BAC/Birmingham Rep); Through the Leaves (Southwark Playhouse/Duchess); Ghost City (Sgript Cymru/Arcola); Witness, Happy Yet (Gate).
Opera includes: Hagoromo, Thimble Rigging (Queen Elizabeth Hall); Jerwood Jazz Solos with Light (Wapping Power Station); A Midsummer Night's Dream (Broomhill Opera).
Dance includes: eight-year collaboration with Richard Alston (Sadler's Wells & tour); Matthew Hawkins (Linbury Studio, ROH); Rosemary Butcher (Queen Elizabeth Hall & European tour); Aletta Collins (Tour); Martin Lawrance (The Place).

Calum Callaghan
For the Royal Court: Food Chain, Young Writers Festival.
Other theatre includes: The Straits (Paines Ploug Traverse/Hampstead); Whistle Down the Wind (Sydmonton Festival); Oliver (Palladium); Les Miserables (Palace); Hey Mr Producer (Lyceum).
Television includes: Heartbeat, Stitch Up, Wall of Silence, The Bill, The Tiny Living Channel, I am a R Gypsy Girl, Writing & Pictures, Black Hearts in Battersea, Children in Need, Hale & Pace.
Film includes: Love Honour & Obey.
Radio includes: The Parting, The Pool.

Emma Dunton (ATC executive producer)
Since joining ATC in 2001 Emma has produced In the Solitude of Cotton Fields by Bernard-Marie Koltes, Arabian Night by Roland Schimmelpfennig, Out of Our Heads by Susan Earl and Janice Phayr One Minute by Simon Stephens and Excuses! by Joan Joel and Jordi Sanchez. Emma has also worke at Volcano Theatre Company producing and managing the national and international tours of Macbeth Director's Cut, The Town That Went Ma and Private Lives. Previously she has worked at th British Council and on low-budget feature films ir Los Angeles.

Laura Elphinstone
Laura has just graduated from Guildhall School of Music & Drama. This is her professional debut.

Soutra Gilmour (designer)
Theatre includes: Antigone (Citizens Theatre, Glasgow); Peter Pan (Tramway, Glasgow); The Birthday Party (Crucible, Sheffield); The Mayor of Zalamea (Everyman, Liverpool); Fool For Love (ETT); Macbeth (English Shakespeare Co); Hand ii Hand (Hampstead); Modern Dance for Beginners (Soho); Animal (The Red Room); Tear from a Glas Eye, Les Justes, Ion, Witness and the Flu Season (Gate); Sun is Shining (BAC Critics' Choice Seaso 59E59, NY); The Women who Swallowed a Pin, Winter's Tale (Southwark Playhouse); When the World was Green (Young Vic); Ghost City (59E59 NY); The Shadow of a Boy (RNT); Through the Leaves (Southwark Playhouse/Duchess).
Opera includes: Coker, Weill, Bernstein (Opera Group, Buxton); Girl of Sand (Almeida Opera); Everyman (Norwich Festival); Eight Songs for a M King (world tour); El Cimmaron (Queen Elizabeth Hall); Twice Through the Heart (Cheltenham Festival); Bathtime (ENO); A Better Place (ENO, London Coliseum).

Sally Hawkins
Theatre includes: The Way of the World (Wilton Music Hall); Misconceptions (Octagon, Bolton); A Midsummer Night's Dream, Much Ado About Nothing (Regent's Park); Pera Palas (NT Studio); The Cherry Orchard, Romeo & Juliet (Theatre Royal, York); The Dybbuk, Accidental Death of an Anarchist (BAC); Svejk (Gate, London); The Whore of Babylon (Globe Education Centre); As You Like It (Buckingham Palace Gala).
Television includes: The Young Visitors, Little Britain, Bunk Bed Boys, Byron, Promoted to Glory, Tipping the Velvet, Casualty.
Film includes: Vera Drake, Layer Cake, All or Nothing.

Steve Marmion (assistant director)
Theatre includes: Edward Gant's Amazing Feats of Loneliness (Theatre Royal, Plymouth); The Horrible History of Christmas (Sherman Theatre).
As director theatre includes: 97 - A play about the Victims of Hillsborough (Edinburgh Festival); Rhinoceros (Chapter Arts); The Visit (Sherman Theatre); Madam Butterfly's Child (Greenwich Festival, London One Act Theatre Festival); SK8 (Theatre Royal, Plymouth); Team Spirit (RNT/ Theatre Royal, Plymouth); Miranda's Magic Mirror (Stephen Joseph Theatre).

Lee Ross
For the Royal Court: Hammett's Apprentice, Some Voices, The Lights, Children's Day.
Other theatre includes: M.A.D., Christmas (Bush); Bugsy Malone (Her Majesty's); Spookhouse (Hampstead); The Neighbour (RNT); Tape (New Venture, Brighton).
Television includes: The Hustle, Dunkirk, The Catherine Tate Show, Trial & Retribution, Amongst Barbarians, The Guilty, Shine on Harvey Moon, The Negotiator, Pressgang, Playing the Field.
Film includes: Secrets & Lies, The English Patient, Rogue Trader, Metroland, Dreaming of Joseph Lees, Vigo - A Passion for Life, ID, Hard Men, Dockers, Sweet Nothing, Island on Bird Street, Secret Society.

Julian Swales (composer)
Julian Swales was the guitarist in 90s alt rock band Kitchens of Distinction and toured with them extensively in the United States. He concentrated on studio-based composition in the late 90s and now writes mainly for film, television, theatre and contemporary dance. Julian's latest work includes Coma, a documentary for Channel 4, and Mummy: The Inside Story, a 3D movie currently showing at the British Museum. Capsule, A Kitchens of Distinction retrospective, was released last year.

aTC

ATC was founded in 1979 to tour innovative work throughout the UK. Over the years the company has developed a tradition of ensemble excellence and a reputation for originality and internationalism, picking up many awards along the way. Since Gordon Anderson and Emma Dunton joined the company in 2001 ATC has focused on contemporary work and forged dynamic partnerships with companies and artists from across the world.

ATC recently worked with Simon Stephens developing ONE MINUTE in a co-production with Sheffield Crucible Theatre. The production went on a national tour before arriving at the Bush Theatre in London in February 2004. Other recent productions include the English language premiere of EXCUSES! by Jordi Sanchez and Joel Joan directed by David Grindley (in a co-production with the Barcelona-based company Krampack) and ARABIAN NIGHT by Roland Schimmelpfennig (in association with Soho Theatre). ATC has also worked with comedy writer-performers SUSAN & JANICE developing their hit show OUT OF OUR HEADS and produced Bernard Marie Koltes' IN THE SOLITUDE OF COTTON FIELDS in a site-specific performance at the disused Aldwych Underground station on the Strand.

Later in 2004 ATC will be producing the UK premiere of German play JEFF KOONS by Rainald Goetz. This production is supported by the Linbury Trust, with a design by Becs Andrews which was awarded Overall Winner of the 2003 Linbury Biennial Prize for Stage Design.

'Anderson's sensitive, precise direction has paid off brilliantly here...the meticulous acting is as persuasive as the direction.'
The Times ***** (One Minute)

Administrator: Jenni Kershaw

ATC, Malvern House, 15-16 Nassau Street, London W1W 7AB
T: 020 7735 8311 F: 020 7735 1031
E: atc@atc-online.com www. atc-online.com

ATC is funded by Arts Council England

JEFF KOONS
by Rainald Goetz
Translated by
David Tushingham

Directed by Gordon Anderson
Designed by Becs Andrews
Movement Director Dan O'Neill

UK TOUR AND LONDON
SEPT-NOV 2004

www.atc-online.com

THE ENGLISH STAGE COMPANY AT THE ROYAL COURT

The English Stage Company at the Royal Court opened in 1956 as a subsidised theatre producing new British plays, international plays and some classical revivals.

The first artistic director George Devine aimed to create a writers' theatre, 'a place where the dramatist is acknowledged as the fundamental creative force in the theatre and where the play is more important than the actors, the director, the designer'. The urgent need was to find a contemporary style in which the play, the acting, direction and design are all combined. He believed that 'the battle will be a long one to continue to create the right conditions for writers to work in'.

Devine aimed to discover 'hard-hitting, uncompromising writers whose plays are stimulating, provocative and exciting'. The Royal Court production of John Osborne's Look Back in Anger in May 1956 is now seen as the decisive starting point of modern British drama and the policy created a new generation of British playwrights. The first wave included John Osborne, Arnold Wesker, John Arden, Ann Jellicoe, N F Simpson and Edward Bond. Early seasons included new international plays by Bertolt Brecht, Eugène Ionesco, Samuel Beckett, Jean-Paul Sartre and Marguerite Duras.

The theatre started with the 400-seat proscenium arch Theatre Downstairs, and in 1969 opened a second theatre, the 60-seat studio Theatre Upstairs. Some productions transfer to the West End, such as Terry Johnson's Hitchcock Blonde, Caryl Churchill's Far Away, Conor McPherson's The Weir, Kevin Elyot's Mouth to Mouth and My Night With Reg. The Royal Court also co-produces plays which have transferred to the West End or toured internationally, such as Sebastian Barry's The Steward of Christendom and Mark Ravenhill's Shopping and Fucking (with Out of Joint), Martin McDonagh's The Beauty Queen Of Leenane (with Druid Theatre Company), Ayub Khan Din's East is East (with Tamasha Theatre Company, and now a feature film).

Since 1994 the Royal Court's artistic policy has again been vigorously directed to finding and producing a new generation of playwrights. The writers include Joe Penhall, Rebecca Prichard, Michael Wynne, Nick Grosso, Judy Upton, Meredith Oakes, Sarah Kane, Anthony Neilson, Judith Johnson, James Stock, Jez Butterworth, Marina Carr, Phyllis Nagy, Simon Block, Martin McDonagh, Mark Ravenhill, Ayub Khan Din, Tamantha Hammerschlag, Jess Walters, Ché Walker, Conor McPherson,

photo: Andy Chopping

Simon Stephens, Richard Bean, Roy Williams, Gary Mitchell, Mick Mahoney, Rebecca Gilman, Christopher Shinn, Kia Corthron, David Gieselmann, Marius von Mayenburg, David Eldridge, Leo Butler, Zinnie Harris, Grae Cleugh, Enda Walsh, Marcos Barbosa, Roland Schimmelpfennig, DeObia Oparei, Vassily Sigarev, the Presnyakov Brothers and Lucy Prebble. This expanded programme of new plays has been made possible through the support of ASK Theater Projects and the Skirball Foundation, The Jerwood Charity, the American Friends of the Royal Court Theatre and many in association with the Royal National Theatre Studio.

In recent years there have been record-breaking productions at the box office, with capacity houses for Roy Williams' Fallout, Terry Johnson's Hitchcock Blonde, Caryl Churchill's A Number, Jez Butterworth's The Night Heron, Rebecca Gilman's Boy Gets Girl, Kevin Elyot's Mouth to Mouth, David Hare's My Zinc Bed and Conor McPherson's The Weir, which transferred to the West End in October 1998 and ran for nearly two years at the Duke of York's Theatre.

The newly refurbished theatre in Sloane Square opened in February 2000, with a policy still inspired by the first artistic director George Devine. The Royal Court is an international theatre for new plays and new playwrights, and the work shapes contemporary drama in Britain and overseas.

AWARDS FOR ROYAL COURT

Jez Butterworth won the 1995 George Devine Award, the Writers' Guild New Writer of the Year Award, the Evening Standard Award for Most Promising Playwright and the Olivier Award for Best Comedy for Mojo.

The Royal Court was the overall winner of the 1995 Prudential Award for the Arts for creativity, excellence, innovation and accessibility. The Royal Court Theatre Upstairs won the 1995 Peter Brook Empty Space Award for innovation and excellence in theatre.

Michael Wynne won the 1996 Meyer-Whitworth Award for The Knocky. Martin McDonagh won the 1996 George Devine Award, the 1996 Writers' Guild Best Fringe Play Award, the 1996 Critics' Circle Award and the 1996 Evening Standard Award for Most Promising Playwright for The Beauty Queen of Leenane. Marina Carr won the 19th Susan Smith Blackburn Prize (1996/7) for Portia Coughlan. Conor McPherson won the 1997 George Devine Award, the 1997 Critics' Circle Award and the 1997 Evening Standard Award for Most Promising Playwright for The Weir. Ayub Khan Din won the 1997 Writers' Guild Awards for Best West End Play and Writers' Guild New Writer of the Year and the 1996 John Whiting Award for East is East (co-production with Tamasha).

At the 1998 Tony Awards, Martin McDonagh's The Beauty Queen of Leenane (co-production with Druid Theatre Company) won four awards including Garry Hynes for Best Director and was nominated for a further two. Eugene Ionesco's The Chairs (co-production with Theatre de Complicite) was nominated for six Tony awards. David Hare won the 1998 Time Out Live Award for Outstanding Achievement and six awards in New York including the Drama League, Drama Desk and New York Critics Circle Award for Via Dolorosa. Sarah Kane won the 1998 Arts Foundation Fellowship in Playwriting. Rebecca Prichard won the 1998 Critics' Circle Award for Most Promising Playwright for Yard Gal (co-production with Clean Break).

Conor McPherson won the 1999 Olivier Award for Best New Play for The Weir. The Royal Court won the 1999 ITI Award for Excellence in International Theatre. Sarah Kane's Cleansed was judged Best Foreign Language Play in 1999 by Theater Heute in Germany. Gary Mitchell won the 1999 Pearson Best Play Award for Trust. Rebecca Gilman was joint winner of the 1999 George Devine Award and won the 1999 Evening Standard Award for Most Promising Playwright for The Glory of Living.

In 1999, the Royal Court won the European theatre prize New Theatrical Realities, presented at Taormina Arte in Sicily, for its efforts in recent years in discovering and producing the work of young British dramatists.

Roy Williams and Gary Mitchell were joint winners of the George Devine Award 2000 for Most Promising Playwright for Lift Off and The Force of Change respectively. At the Barclays Theatre Awards 2000 presented by the TMA, Richard Wilson won the Best Director Award for David Gieselmann's Mr Kolpert and Jeremy Herbert won the Best Designer Award for Sarah Kane's 4.48 Psychosis. Gary Mitchell won the Evening Standard's Charles Wintour Award 2000 for Most Promising Playwright for The Force of Change. Stephen Jeffreys' I Just Stopped by to See the Man won an AT&T: On Stage Award 2000.

David Eldridge's Under the Blue Sky won the Time Out Live Award 2001 for Best New Play in the West End. Leo Butler won the George Devine Award 2001 for Most Promising Playwright for Redundant. Roy Williams won the Evening Standard's Charles Wintour Award 2001 for Most Promising Playwright for Clubland. Grae Cleugh won the 2001 Olivier Award for Most Promising Playwright for Fucking Games. Richard Bean was joint winner of the George Devine Award 2002 for Most Promising Playwright for Under the Whaleback. Caryl Churchill won the 2002 Evening Standard Award for Best New Play for A Number. Vassily Sigarev won the 2002 Evening Standard Charles Wintour Award for Most Promising Playwright for Plasticine. Ian MacNeil won the 2002 Evening Standard Award for Best Design for A Number and Plasticine. Peter Gill won the 2002 Critics' Circle Award for Best New Play for The York Realist (English Touring Theatre). Ché Walker won the 2003 George Devine Award for Most Promising Playwright for Flesh Wound. Lucy Prebble won the 2003 Critics' Circle Award and the 2004 George Devine Award for Most Promising Playwright for The Sugar Syndrome.

ROYAL COURT BOOKSHOP

The Royal Court bookshop offers a diverse selection of contemporary plays and publications on the theory and practice of modern drama. The staff specialise in assisting with the selection of audition monologues and scenes.
Royal Court playtexts from past and present productions cost £2.
The Bookshop is situated in the downstairs ROYAL COURT BAR AND FOOD.
Monday–Friday 3–10pm, Saturday 2–10pm
For information tel: 020 7565 5024
or email: bookshop@royalcourttheatre.com

PROGRAMME SUPPORTERS

The Royal Court (English Stage Company Ltd) receives its principal funding from Arts Council England, London. It is also supported financially by a wide range of private companies and public bodies and earns the remainder of its income from the box office and its own trading activities. The Royal Borough of Kensington & Chelsea gives an annual grant to the Royal Court Young Writers Programme.
The Genesis Foundation supports the International Season and Young Writers Festival.

The Jerwood Charity supports new plays by new playwrights through the Jerwood New Playwrights series. The Skirball Foundation funds a Playwrights' Programme at the theatre. The Artistic Director's Chair is supported by a lead grant from The Peter Jay Sharp Foundation, contributing to the activities of the Artistic Director's office. Bloomberg Mondays, the Royal Court's reduced price ticket scheme, is supported by Bloomberg. Over the past eight years the BBC has supported the Gerald Chapman Fund for directors.

ROYAL COURT
SLOANE SQUARE

AUTUMN 2004

Jerwood Theatre Downstairs

NEW PLAYS BY
JOE PENHALL
AND KEVIN ELYOT

Jerwood Theatre Upstairs

YOUNG
WRITERS
FESTIVAL 2004

A Genesis Project

Full details published July 2004

BOX OFFICE
020 7565 5000
BOOK ONLINE
www.royalcourttheatre.com

JERWOOD
NEW PLAYWRIGHTS

Since 1993 Jerwood New Playwrights has contributed to 46 new plays at the Royal Court including Joe Penhall's SOME VOICES, Mark Ravenhill's SHOPPING AND FUCKING (co-production with Out of Joint), Ayub Khan Din's EAST IS EAST (co-production with Tamasha), Martin McDonagh's THE BEAUTY QUEEN OF LEENANE (co-production with Druid Theatre Company), Conor McPherson's THE WEIR, Nick Grosso's REAL CLASSY AFFAIR, Sarah Kane's 4.48 PSYCHOSIS, Gary Mitchell's THE FORCE OF CHANGE, David Eldridge's UNDER THE BLUE SKY, David Harrower's PRESENCE, Simon Stephens' HERONS, Roy Williams' CLUBLAND, Leo Butler's REDUNDANT, Michael Wynne's THE PEOPLE ARE FRIENDLY, David Greig's OUTLYING ISLANDS, Zinne Harris' NIGHTINGALE AND CHASE, Grae Cleugh's FUCKING GAMES, Rona Munro's IRON, Richard Bean's UNDER THE WHALEBACK, Ché Walker's FLESH WOUND, Roy Williams' FALLOUT, Mick Mahoney's FOOD CHAIN, and Ayub Khan Din's NOTES ON FALLING LEAVES.

This season Jerwood New Playwrights are supporting LUCKY DOG by Leo Butler and COUNTRY MUSIC by Simon Stephens.

The Jerwood Charity is a registered charity dedicated to imaginative and responsible funding and sponsorship of the arts, education, design and other areas of human endeavour and excellence.

Ayun Khan Din's NOTES ON FALLING LEAVES
(photo: Alastair Muir)

Leo Butler's LUCKY DOG
(photo: Ivan Kyncl)

Country Music

Characters

Jamie Carris, eighteen/twenty-nine/thirty-nine
Matty Carris, nineteen
Emma Carris, seventeen
Lynsey Sergeant, fifteen

Setting

The play takes place in Thurrock, Essex; Her Majesty's Prison Grendon, Buckinghamshire; and Durham Road, Sunderland, between 1983 and 2004.

– denotes interruption or a sudden halt

. . . denotes a trailing off

This play is dedicated to those teachers and writers I worked with in HMP Wandsworth and HMP Grendon and YOT Salford and YOT Kensington and Chelsea between 2001 and 2003.

I am indebted to Ian Rickson, Graham Whybrow, Marianne Elliott and Mel Kenyon as well as to all the staff and writers of the Young Writers' programme at the Royal Court for their support while I was writing this play. And Stanley. And Oscar. And Poll.

S.S., June 2004

One

Friday 14 July 1983, 2 a.m.

A parked Ford Cortina in the car park of a service garage on the A13 east of Thurrock.

Jamie Carris, *eighteen years old, sits in the driver's seat. He is drinking coffee from a paper cup.*

Lynsey Sergeant, *fifteen years old, sits in the passenger seat.*

Jamie   You reckon they will?

Lynsey   Yeah.

Jamie   Check the beds?

Lynsey   Always do now. New night warden. Does bed checks. Window checks. Everything.

Jamie   Reckon they'll suss yer?

Lynsey   Course.

He starts chuckling. She joins in after a while.

Jamie   What'll they do?

Lynsey   I don't know. Go mad prob'ly. Crack up. Have a fucking eppy. Call the old bill.

Jamie   Will they?

Lynsey   I dunno. Sometimes do. Sometimes can't be arsed.

She sits forward in the passenger seat. Staring hard out of the front window.

Jamie *turns to look at her.*

Jamie   You cold?

Lynsey   No.

Jamie   You want my jumper?

Lynsey   I'm all right.

Jamie   You're funny.

Lynsey   Why?

Jamie   Look at yer.

Lynsey   What about me?

Jamie (*smiles*)   Nothing. (*Drinks. Holds cup in his teeth. Grins at her.*) You hungry?

Lynsey   No, I'm all right.

Jamie   You want a packet of crisps? I've got fucking hundreds.

He reaches behind his seat to the back seat and pulls out a squashed multi-pack of crisps. Starts to rifle through the different packets.

Lynsey (*laughs at the amount of crisps*)   No, thank you. Honestly. I'm all right.

Jamie   All fucking flavours and all. Salt and vinegar. Cheese and onion. Beef. Here. Have one.

Lynsey   Bad for yer, them. Rot yer teeth.

Jamie   Fuck off.

Lynsey   Make yer fat.

Jamie   No they won't. Have one.

Lynsey   No.

She sticks her tongue out at him

Jamie   Starve to death, you. I'm meant to look after you. You'll waste away. (*Beat.*) Anyway. (*Grins at her.*) I like a bit of fat, me.

Lynsey   Jamie.

Jamie   I do. Bit of a tummy.

He opens his packet. Takes a mouthful.

Lynsey   You think I'm fat?

Jamie No. Just saying. Should have one.

Pause.

I like prawn cocktail best.

Lynsey (*imitating*) 'I like prawn cocktail best.'

He laughs at her. Bounces himself as far forward as her in his seat.

Jamie That was fucking great. Weren't it, Lynse? Weren't that fucking smart?

Lynsey *starts to chuckle slightly.*

Lynsey Yeah.

Jamie (*acting out his driving with his right hand*) Fucking hand-break turns. Bouff. Nnnyyyeeeoowwww. Give it! Fucking tell yer.

Lynsey *laughs at him.*

Jamie Mad fucking Max, mate. Fucking Rambo,

Lynsey Dickhead.

Jamie You wait till they finish the motorway, Lynse. Gonna build a big old bridge, and everything. See us then, tell yer, I'll be fucking dynamite. (*Beat.*) You done the old tunnel before?

Lynsey The what?

Jamie Going south, out of Thurrock, you ever done that?

Lynsey No.

Jamie Should do. It's quality. I do it. Bomb it. Fucking overtaking and everything.

Lynsey You're full of shit, you.

Jamie Am not.

Lynsey Yer've never done that.

Jamie Yes I have.

Lynsey   How come yer never took us, then?

Jamie   Never wanted to. Yer whinge too much.

Lynsey   Shut it, you.

Jamie *laughs. Sits back down. Puts his feet up on the steering wheel.*

Jamie   You comfy?

Lynsey   Yeah.

Jamie   You sure?

Lynsey   Yeah.

Jamie   Put your seat back.

Lynsey   I said I'm all right, didn't I?

Jamie   You gonna go sleep?

Lynsey   Might do in a bit. I'm all right for now.

Jamie   Should do. Just go to sleep whenever you want.
I don't mind driving with people asleep. Some people can't
do it. Doesn't bother me. I only need a little bit of a break.
Won't be long. Have a quick break and we'll crack on.

He pulls a bottle of tequila from under his seat and necks a mouthful.

You want some of this, Lynsey?

Lynsey   No, thanks. I'm all right.

Jamie (*coughs, half giggles*)   Should have some. Fucking does
the business. Telling yer.

Lynsey   You reckon?

Jamie   Hits the fucking, the spot, the. Tell yer. Hits it.
Bang. Like that.

Lynsey   Shouldn't drink and drive.

Jamie   Fuck off.

Lynsey   Should yer, though?

Jamie   I'm all right. I'm better, me, with a bit of a drink. I see stuff clearer.

Lynsey   Psycho.

Jamie   Bit of coffee and that. Bit of Coke. I'm away.

Lynsey *watches as he slugs another tequila. Puts the bottle back and pulls a can of Coke from under the same seat. Opens it.*

Jamie   When we get there. I'm going doing the laundrettes, Lynsey. You coming?

Lynsey   The laundrettes?

Jamie   Go down Poynter's Lane. Sutton Road. Get some cash.

Lynsey   How?

Jamie   Just smash up the coin slots. Get a crowbar. It's easy. Nobody says anything.

Lynsey   Could do.

Jamie   Get some chips, couldn't we, for our tea?

Lynsey   Where we staying?

Jamie   I'm gonna get us a hotel.

Lynsey   Are yer?

Jamie   Get one on the sea front. Be fucking smart.

Lynsey   I've never been Southend before.

Jamie   Ain't yer?

Lynsey   No.

Jamie   It's quality. Swear. Better than fucking Margate.

Lynsey   You got some money for a hotel, Jamie?

Jamie   Course. It'll be sound.

Offers her the can.

You want some Coke?

Lynsey   No, thank you. I'm all right.

Jamie *finishes his drink. Starts chuckling.*

Jamie   Guess who I'm thinking about?

Lynsey   Who?

Jamie   No, go on, have a guess.

Lynsey   Fuck off, Jamie, who?

Jamie   Mr Mackenzie.

Lynsey (*laughing*)   You should have seen him.

Jamie   I can imagine. Mad bird, you.

Slight pause.

It's funny. If he saw us, I wonder what he'd think.

Lynsey   I don't know.

Jamie   Probably think. Probably think. Probably think, yeah. That's fucking typical. I am not surprised one fucking second. Don't yer reckon?

Lynsey   Probably get dead jealous. Wish he was doing it too.

Jamie *smiles at her.*

A slight pause.

Lynsey   Don't spend too much money. On the hotel. Will yer?

Jamie   No. Don't panic. Just get a nice one. Nice B & B or summit.

Lynsey   You gonna get a job, Jamie?

Jamie   Course.

Lynsey   What job you gonna get, you think?

Jamie   Fucking, a good one.

Lynsey   Could we get a flat, you reckon? After a bit?

Jamie Yeah. Or a house. If we move out a little bit. Get a little house.

Lynsey Get a garden.

Jamie Could do. Be good, wouldn't it?

Lynsey Be fucking great.

A slight pause.

Lynsey What time is it now?

Jamie Quarter past two.

Lynsey Funny. I'm not tired at all.

Jamie You should try and sleep, though. You'll feel better for it.

Beat.

Lynsey Where did you get the car?

Jamie Up Valley Parade.

Lynsey It's good i'n't it?

Jamie I think it's great.

Lynsey I like the headrests. They're well comfy.

She leans her head back on hers to test it.

Jamie I was gonna ask you something.

Lynsey What?

Jamie In a bit. Not for a while. Not for years maybe. You think Matty could come stay with us?

Lynsey Yeah.

Jamie Be good, wouldn't it, if he did? When he's older and that.

Lynsey Be great. I like Matty.

Jamie Can be a bit of a little dick at times but he's not too bad normally.

Lynsey   He's only eight.

Jamie   Yeah.

Lynsey   He's eight, you're eighteen, Jamie. Course you think he's a dick. (*Beat.*) I think he's quite sweet.

Jamie   Be like having a kid.

Lynsey   Fuck off.

Jamie (*smirks*)   I might get another coffee.

Lynsey   All right.

Jamie   Then I think we should maybe fuck off.

Lynsey   Right.

Jamie   Should only take an hour. Max. If we put a bit of speed on.

Lynsey   Right. Good. Jamie . . .

Jamie   Yeah?

Lynsey   You reckon your mum'll notice you've gone?

Jamie   I dunno. Maybe. (*He chuckles.*) Fucking psycho. Sick of her.

Lynsey   You reckon they'll be looking for yer?

Jamie   Who?

Lynsey   Filth.

Jamie   I don't know.

Lynsey   Be looking for the car, though, won't they?

Jamie   I don't know. I don't reckon they bother any more. About cars and that.

Lynsey   I think they will.

Jamie   They'll start looking south, though. Bet yer. They'll go down Margate. Won't think about crossing the river. Will they? Won't think about that. They're not smart.

Lynsey   Did you kill him?

Jamie (*splutters a laugh*)   Did I what?

Lynsey   Gary Noolan. Did you kill him, do yer think?

Jamie (*still laughing*)   Oh for fuck's sake, Lynsey.

Lynsey   Did yer, Jamie?

Jamie (*still*)   Course I didn't kill him. Fucking. I only. 'Did you kill him.' Yer monghead.

Lynsey   Well, I don't know, do I? Might have done. Do my head in if you did.

Jamie   Well, I didn't. So just.

Lynsey   You reckon you're gonna get sent down?

Jamie   You what?

Lynsey   Last time they said you might go Borstal. Go East Sussex.

Jamie *laughs at her.*

Lynsey   I'm just worried about you.

Jamie   Well, just don't be.

Lynsey   Jamie. I don't even know what you did. Not properly. You just turn up. Beep your fucking horn. 'Get in. We're fucking off.' I'm like, 'All right, Jamie. Nice car.'

Jamie   I told you.

Lynsey   No you never.

Jamie   I went down Stationers. Looking for Gary Noolan. After he'd left ours. After he'd left our mum's. After I saw you. And I found him. And I glassed the cunt. I went down the offie. Wanted some fags. And a bottle of tequila. And some crisps. Didn't have any money. This kid started getting lippy. So I stabbed him. Took all the stuff. Went outside. (*About the car.*) Found this cunt down Valley Parade. Came and found you. I thought you'd be happy.

Lynsey   You never told me about the kid.

Jamie   You what?

Lynsey   You never did.

Jamie   It's not a big deal.

Lynsey   How old was he?

Jamie   Fucksake.

Lynsey   How old was he, Jamie?

Jamie   What does it matter?

Lynsey   Matters to me.

Jamie   I don't know. I don't know how old he was. Sixteen.

Lynsey   Right.

Jamie *pulls the tequila out again and slugs some. Wipes his mouth. Stares at her. Smiles at her.*

Jamie   Do you want a bit of this?

Offers the tequila.

Lynsey   Yeah.

Takes the tequila. Wipes the neck. Drinks.

Jamie   Do you want some crisps?

Offers the multi-pack again.

Lynsey   Yeah.

Jamie   Got cheese and onion. Salt and vinegar. Beef. Roast chicken. Ready salted.

Lynsey   Salt and vinegar.

Jamie   Here.

Lynsey   Thanks.

Lynsey *takes a packet of crisps and opens it. They eat. Short time.*

Lynsey I reckon they will find you.

A slight pause.

I just thought I'd say that.

A slight pause. **Jamie** *sits forward again, eyes lit up.*

Jamie *sniggers.*

Jamie Should we do a house?

Lynsey What?

Jamie Us two. Go and do a house. When we get up Southend. Find a big one, one of the big houses there. Up seafront. Wakering Road. You should see them. They've got fucking everything.

Lynsey Stop it.

Jamie Hi-fis. Videos. Posh carpets. The works. We'd make a packet. Do a piss. Do a shit on the floor. I'm gonna do that, I reckon.

Lynsey Stop it, Jamie.

Jamie Stop what?

Lynsey You know.

Jamie No. Stop what? Stop what, Lynsey? Stop what? Come on. Fucking hell!

He thumps the dashboard.

Pause.

Lynsey *clocks him before she speaks.*

Lynsey What'd happen to Matty?

Jamie You what?

Lynsey If you got sent down. What'd happen to Matty? Who'd look after him? Your mum?

Jamie He'd be all right.

Lynsey   Can I tell you something?

Jamie   I'd –

Lynsey   I think you're wrong about the cops.

Jamie   You what?

Lynsey   I think they'll be looking for you. I think they'll know to look for the car and I think they'll know that you've been the one who's nicked it. I don't think they're as thick as you think they are.

Jamie   Don't you?

Lynsey   If you went back, hand yerself, write a statement, a, a, a confession or something.

Jamie   Do what?

Lynsey   I think might make a difference.

Jamie   Fuck off.

Lynsey   To the way they treat you.

Jamie   Fuck off.

Lynsey   To your sentence or, or, or –

Jamie   Fuck off Lynsey. Fuck off. Just fuck off, would you? Christ!

Lynsey   I'm right, aren't I?

Jamie   No.

Lynsey   I am. Course I am. You know I am.

Jamie   –

Lynsey   I want to go home.

Jamie   Oh!

Lynsey   I want to go back to the home.

Jamie   You got to be kidding.

Lynsey   I wanna go back to Clarence House, I'm worried about what they'll say.

Jamie   Swear. Lynsey.

Lynsey   It's all right for you, Jamie. I ain't got nowhere else to go.

Jamie   Look at me.

Lynsey   They've not been as bad to me as they were to you.

Jamie   Do you know what would happen?

Lynsey   I don't care.

Jamie   You can't. You can't go. You can't go home. You can't.

Lynsey   I'm going.

Jamie   You want me to smack yer? Do yer? 'Cause I will. I fucking will.

Lynsey   You what?

Jamie   I'll smack yer face.

Lynsey   Don't you talk to me like that.

Jamie   I fucking don't believe you, Lynsey, Christ.

Lynsey   Think you're so hard.

Jamie   Don't you push it.

Lynsey   You fucking do, though. Think yer the big man. Yer fucking not. Yer fucking just –

Jamie *hits her head with the ball of his open palm.*

Lynsey   Ow. That hurt me.

Jamie *does it again. Makes her hit her head against the side of the car.*

Lynsey   Get off.

Jamie   Fuck you.

He does it again. She starts crying.

Jamie   Stop crying. Stop crying. Stop fucking crying. What they gonna say now? Eh? Fucking cunts. Clarence House. Fucking. You should see your face.

Lynsey *tries the door.*

It's locked. Don't try it 'cause it's fucking locked.

Long pause.

Lynsey *wipes her eyes.*

Lynsey   Take me home, please.

Jamie   Fuck off.

Lynsey   Please, Jamie.

Jamie   Fuck off.

Lynsey   I'll get back anyway. Go on the fucking train. I'll tell 'em you hit us if you don't. Tell 'em all. Tell Ross Mack.

Jamie (*beat first*)   You wouldn't.

Lynsey   Things he did to you. Jamie. He'd do 'em again if I asked him to. Mad boy, that one. Do anything I tell him.

Jamie   You fucking wouldn't.

Lynsey   You could always hang yerself again, Jamie, eh? (*Beat.*) I wouldn't lift yer down next time.

She looks at him.

Slight pause.

Jamie *looks out of the side window.*

Lynsey   Fucking hotel. Are you mental or what? How would you, couldn't even sign in. Could yer? Thick cunt. Big spastic.

Slight pause.

Jamie *bites his bottom lip.*

Jamie   Go to sleep.

Lynsey   You're joking, aren't yer?

Jamie   Ruined it now.

Lynsey   Please let me out of the car.

Jamie   You not talking to us now? Is that it?

Lynsey   I hate you now.

Jamie   I don't know what you hate me for 'cause this is all your fault.

Lynsey   You what?

Jamie   Could have come up earlier on. Could have come this afternoon. Straight after I saw 'em. Straight after you came out. If you didn't want to go back Clarence House.

Pause.

I even asked yer. Didn't I? Didn't I, though?

Long pause. **Lynsey** *turns away from him.*

Jamie *drinks some more Coke.*

Lights another cigarette. Smokes it.

Jamie   Ross Mack's a fucking pussy.

Finishes his cigarette. Takes as long as it takes him to smoke it.

Winds down his window and throws it out.

Please stay with us.

Slight pause.

I'm sorry I hit you.

Slight pause.

I'm sorry I hit you, Lynsey, please stay with us.

Slight pause.

It never hurt yer, did it?

He goes to stroke her. **Lynsey** *winces away at first, but then lets him stroke her hair.*

Lynsey   Course it fucking hurt me, you thick bastard.

Jamie   I reckon we could get away, y'know? I reckon we could. Dump this car. Get another. Fuck right off. We could go up Scotland or something. The two of us. You looking after us. Me doing driving and that. Couldn't we, Lynsey? Don't yer reckon?

Lynsey   No.

Jamie   Why not? Why not, though?

Lynsey   I wouldn't want to. We couldn't anyway.

Jamie   We could, though, Lynsey, couldn't we? I reckon we could. I reckon it'd be fucking easy, Lynse. Be a piece of piss, mate. It'd be all right.

Lynsey   Jamie –

Jamie   Fucking hell!

Lynsey   You're not thinking.

Jamie   I am so thinking. I am thinking like, like, like, like. Please.

Lynsey   No.

Jamie   Yer gonna make me do it on my own, Lynsey? 'Cause I will.

Lynsey   Should have thought about that. Shouldn't yer? Shouldn't you?

Jamie *looks away from her. Gathers his breath. Holds his head up to the roof of the car. Squeezes his eyes closed tight. Looks back to her. Some time.*

Lynsey   You should go home. All the cops. I think it'd be all right, if you go home.

Jamie   Do yer?

Lynsey   I think it might be.

Jamie *grins. Swigs from the tequila.*

Jamie   Yer ever get like yer wanna cut yer eyes out?

He wipes his mouth with the back of his hand.

Jamie   I remember when I was a kid.

The two stare out, unable to look at one another.

The lights fall.

Two

Tuesday 15 September 1994, 2.15 p.m. The visiting room of Her Majesty's Prison Grendon, Buckinghamshire.

A white table with a blue Formica top. Two blue plastic chairs.

There is a constant noise of echoes. Steel. Shouts. Incoherent. Ever present.

Matty Carris, *nineteen years old, stands above one of the chairs. He has a jacket on over a jumper and black jeans.* **Jamie Carris** *stands across the room from him.* **Jamie** *is wearing a grey sweatshirt, grey sweatpants, and trainers. He is thicker-set than we last saw him. Tougher. More muscular. He is twenty-nine years old. He is in the fifth year of what will be a fourteen-year stretch.*

The two stare at each other for a short while.

Jamie   You have to sit down.

Matty   What?

Jamie   You can't stand up. They have to do checks on you if you touch us. You have to sit down. I'm sorry.

Matty   Right.

Very long pause. The two men examine each other's face and then, led by **Jamie**, *they break into smiles.*

Jamie   Hello, Matty.

Matty   Hello, Jamie.

Jamie   How are you, mate?

Matty   I'm, I'm, I'm.

Jamie   It's good you're here.

Matty   Yeah. I. It's good to see you.

Very long pause. The two of them stare at each other.

It's funny as it goes.

Jamie   What is?

Matty   When I come in. They did a, one of them things, a rub down on us.

Jamie   Oh yeah?

Matty   I got the, the giggles, didn't I? I couldn't help myself. It was ticklish.

Jamie   You fucking Muppet.

Matty   And the more I tried not to. The more I wanted to laugh. Fucking.

Jamie   What you like?

Matty   I know.

Jamie   You should sit down, mate.

Matty   Right.

He does. **Jamie** *sits with him.*

Jamie   Don't panic.

Matty   No. I won't. I'm all right.

Pause. Then **Matty** *nods, smiling encouragement.*

Matty   It's all right here. Innit?

Jamie   What?

Matty   I, when I was coming up. All the, the garden out front. That house and everything.

Jamie   Yeah.

Matty   I thought. Y'know? Looked all right.

Jamie   Yeah.

Matty   You get to do that, do yer?

Jamie   The garden?

Matty   Yeah.

Jamie   Not that one. No. Others.

Matty   Right. That's all right, innit?

Jamie   Yeah. Yeah. It's not bad. It's. That's another nick actually.

Matty   What?

Jamie   It is. There're two. This one. Springhill. Is the other one.

Matty   Bloody hell.

Jamie   Yeah.

Matty   Some places there are no prisons, are there? Here you can't fucking move for them.

Jamie   That's right.

Matty   Yeah.

Jamie   How was your journey?

Matty   Yeah. It was, easy. Y'know?

Jamie   Yeah?

Matty   Nice. Coming up through the country and that. Funny, innit?

Jamie   What?

Matty   The way this place just sits here. Don't notice it. Do yer? Until you're right here.

Jamie   No.

Matty   Takes yer by surprise, kind of, don't it?

Jamie smiles. *Tries to hold his eye contact.* **Matty** *can't.*

Jamie   Five year.

Matty   Yeah.

Jamie   Five years, Matty.

Matty   Yeah.

Jamie   You were thirteen.

Matty   Yeah.

Jamie   You want a cup of tea, mate?

Matty   What?

Jamie   You can get them. You ask them. They'll give you. I could murder a cup. They're like twenty pence or summink.

Matty   I can go.

Jamie   You got any money?

Matty   Yeah. Yeah. Yeah. Yeah.

Jamie   I can make us a, make us a rollie. You want a rollie?

Matty   Yeah. Go on.

Jamie   You go and get the teas and I'll.

Matty   Sure.

Leaves him rolling a cigarette. Hands shaking. Makes two. With real care. It's difficult for him to do this.

After a minute or so **Matty** *returns with two cups of tea in polystyrene cups.*

Matty   Here you are.

Jamie   Beauty.

Beat. **Jamie** *stares at* **Matty**.

Matty   I bought you some tobacco. As it goes. Left it on the, on the, the, the, with the gate. They said it'd be all right.

Jamie   Yeah. They'll drop it over. Thank you.

Matty   And some phone cards I got yer.

Jamie   Right.

Matty   But you can't use them. Or summink. Is that right? You need special ones?

Jamie   Yeah.

Matty   I'll, next time.

Jamie   Yeah.

Jamie *smiles. Beat.*

Jamie   It was good to get your letter.

Matty   Yeah. I should have written sooner.

Jamie   I wish you had.

Matty   I know.

Jamie   I'm not angry or nothing. You were a fucking kid, eh? Can't blame yer for that. I just wish. Yer with me?

Matty   Yeah.

Matty *looks away from him. Tries to smile down into his teacup.*

Jamie   How's Mum?

Matty   She's okay. She's well. She's all right. Yeah. She told me to tell you. She's gonna try and come in. You send her a VO, she'll come in, definitely. She said.

Jamie   Right. Good. She doesn't need to.

Matty   No. She said she wanted to.

Jamie   Right. That's good. How's Al?

Matty   He's all right. Same really. Tell you what.

Jamie   What?

Matty   That, that, that queue. Fucking hell.

Jamie   What?

Matty   Some of them people in the, the, the waiting to come in.

Jamie   Yeah?

Matty   Fuck me. Fucking psychos. Fucking freaks. Worse out there than they are in here, half of them, I reckon.

Jamie *laughs, slurps his tea. Flicks ash.*

Jamie Calm down.

Matty What?

Jamie You. Calm down. It's all right.

Matty I am calm.

Beat.

Jamie Good.

Pause.

Matty It's funny. Standing at the gate. Thinking about all this. Back here. This building, when you're standing outside of it. Looking in. Waiting to come in. Bit fucking . . .

Pause.

I remember when you got out of East Sussex. After you glassed Gary Noolan.

Jamie Oh yeah?

Matty Coming up to meet yer. That was the same.

Pause.

Jamie *drinks his tea. Smiles.*

Matty Is it different here?

Jamie What?

Matty To young offenders?

Jamie (*mouthful of tea*) This place is a bit weird. All the therapy groups.

Matty Right.

Jamie *goes into the pockets of his sweatpants.*

Jamie You want a sweet?

Matty What?

Jamie   I got some sweets, you want one?

Matty   Yeah. Go on then. Ta.

Jamie *passes him a sweet, which he puts in his mouth. The two of them chew for a while.*

Jamie   Can I call you Matt? Not Matty? Is that all right?

Matty   Yeah. Course you can. If you want to. Course.

Jamie   Sounds better. Don't it?

Matty   I don't know. Matt. Yeah. Sounds all right. I don't mind.

Jamie   Sounds better. (*Beat.*) Look at you.

Matty   What?

Jamie   Fucking shoulders on you!

Matty   What?

Jamie   You're like.

Matty   What?

Jamie *smiles. Doesn't answer. Relights his cigarette.*

Jamie   I might be getting day release.

Matty   You what?

Jamie   I might. They said. I'm up for my board next month. There's a possibility.

Matty   Fucking hell.

Jamie   I know.

Matty   That's . . .

Jamie   Come out. Go up London.

Matty   I'd come up and meet you.

Jamie   Be good.

Matty   Yeah.

Jamie   Just to see everybody. Go home.

Matty   Yeah. (*Beat.*) You wanna see the Bridge.

Jamie   They finished it, have they?

Matty   Couple of years back. You'd like it, I reckon.

Beat.

Jamie   How's, how's, how's college? How's college? Everything all right, yeah?

Matty   Yeah. Not bad. You know.

Jamie   What year you in now?

Matty   'S my second year.

Jamie   Second year. Right. And it's going all right, is it?

Matty   It's going. Yeah. I. It's going fine. Actually. Yeah.

Pause.

I was thinking of jacking it in a while back, as it goes.

Jamie   What?

Matty   I was thinking of knocking it on the head. College.

Jamie   Why?

Matty   I don't know really, just –

Jamie   What you wanna do that for? Don't be stupid. As if you wanna go round doing that.

Matty   I got a mate who's, he runs his own company. Does a bit of painting and decorating. Does houses. And bits of, y'know, chippying and that. Bit of bricklaying. He reckoned he could get us steady work. Take us on. Everything. I thought I might go and work with him. (*Beat.*) I might not. I've not decided.

Jamie *looks at him for a while. Sucks air between his teeth. Looks away, round the room at the other visits.*

Matty   What?

Jamie *looks back.*

Jamie   You seen Lynsey much?

Matty   Yeah. Bits.

Jamie   Seen Emma?

Matty   Yeah.

Jamie   How they doing?

Matty   I think they're all right.

Jamie   Are they?

Matty   Yeah.

Jamie   They ain't been in.

Matty   No?

Jamie   Four years.

Matty   Right.

Jamie *starts chewing on the nail of his right thumb as he talks.*

Jamie   It was my idea for them not to. It's not a good thing for a girl who's four. Y'know? She's four years old and they're asking her to take her fucking socks off and having a clock of them.

Matty   Right.

Jamie   So . . . . But they're all right?

Matty   I think they are, Jamie. Yeah.

Jamie   I should stop biting my nails.

Matty   Yeah.

Jamie   Fuckin' disgusting habit, I think.

Smiles.

Pause.

Matty   Jamie, Lynsey's moved up north.

Pause.

She met a bloke.

Pause.

She met some bloke and she moved up north with him and she took Emma with her.

Pause.

Moved up Sunderland.

Pause.

She came to, came to, came to, to tell us. Came round to the house. She wouldn't tell me where she was going exactly but she promised she'd try and phone me. Let us know.

Pause.

It was a month ago.

Pause.

She wanted me to come and see you. To tell you. She isn't going to come and see you herself, she said. She doesn't want Emma to come and see you. She doesn't want that.

Pause.

I never met him. I don't know who he is or what he's like. Or what he does. Or anything.

Pause. **Jamie** *nods over and over.*

Jamie   Right. Right. Right. Right. Right.

Matty   I haven't been able to sleep. Thinking about how I was going to tell you.

Jamie   Right.

Matty   Jamie, I'm really sorry, mate.

Very long pause. Two staring at each other. **Matty** *finds it difficult.*

Jamie   They didn't leave an address?

Matty No.

Jamie Will you ring them, find out?

Matty I can't.

Jamie Ring them, Matt. Somebody must know their number.

Matty Jamie, it's not as . . .

Jamie Not as what? Not as what? Matt? Not as what?

Matty Jamie, don't.

Jamie Don't what? Matt? Come on.

Matty This is difficult for me.

Jamie What is?

Matty This.

Jamie What did you say to her?

Matty I didn't know what to say.

Jamie Didn't yer?

Matty *looks away.*

Pause.

Jamie Five years I done for you.

Matty Don't.

Jamie I haven't seen you. You never wrote to me.

Matty I couldn't.

Jamie I only did it 'cause of you, mate.

Matty Don't say that.

Jamie I come out of East Sussex and you're a fucking child.

Matty I didn't ask you to do nothing.

Jamie And you're swanning round Stone Street with fucking Ross Mack, like you're his little fucking prime piece of pussy! Matty, you have no idea –

Matty I could have sorted him out.

Jamie What he was like. What he could do. What he did to me. The things he did to us. He was a proper nonce, Matty. I come out and he's hanging around you like a, like a, like a –

Matty You didn't need to do what you did.

Jamie And she's telling you *that* and you didn't know what to say to her? Fucking hell!

Matty You can't blame me.

Jamie Don't cry. Not in here.

Matty I'm not crying! (*Beat.*) I wanted to tell you myself. I didn't want you to find out from anybody else.

Jamie Didn't yer?

Matty No.

Jamie Well, that's fucking –

Matty That was important to me.

Pause.

I think about you all the time.

Pause.

Jamie Shake my hand.

No response.

Matt.

Matty *is reluctant.*

Jamie Here. Matt. Shake my hand. Shake my hand, Matt.

He does. **Jamie** *holds* **Matty**'s *hand longer and tighter than* **Matty** *wants him to.*

Jamie   Is that the only reason you came?

Matty   No, course it's not.

Jamie   Is that the only reason you've come in to see me, Matt?

Matty   Jamie, no. It isn't.

Jamie   'Cause if it is.

Matty   It isn't, I swear.

Pause.

Jamie   You know how you sometimes you have to, with a woman, you have to spit in their face, don't you? Because you can't hit a woman, can you? So that's what you have to do. Isn't it, Matt?

Matty   I don't know.

Longer pause. **Jamie** *strokes* **Matt's** *held hand with his free hand.*

Jamie   How's Mum really?

Matty   What?

Jamie   How's Mum really?

Matty   I don't know.

Jamie   They won't let us out. To see her. Isn't gonna happen.

Matty   No.

Jamie   Have you the ability to count to ten? Can you spell your name?

Matty   You what?

Jamie   Nothing. Don't matter.

Jamie *still holds his hand. Long pause.*

The first nick I was in was called **HMP Risley**. They send a lot of lifers there to start their sentence. One night. Two weeks in. I'm on the balcony. In the middle of the wing.

I hear these shouts going out. 'GET BEHIND THE DOORS!
BANG UP! BANG UP! NOW!' Whole landing's clear of
cons in two minutes. When that happens you know something's gonna go. I look out. I'm trying to clock what's going
down. There are seven or eight screws positioning themselves
outside a cell on the landing below mine. There's this woman,
woman officer, opens the flap on the door. And you can
only just hear her talking inside. She unlocks the door.
Draws her whistle. Which you don't do. 'Cause they're for
fucking, for, for, for emergency. And she blows it. And they
pile in. Seven or eight of them. And what they do is they
start beating the fuck out of this, what I find out later, is a,
a, a boy. The fucking screams from him. They break his
hand. Bash it against the door. He's screaming for, for, for
minutes. And the thing is. He keeps apologising. Keeps
promising over and over to be good. And she's giving it
'Break his arm! Break his arm!'

Long pause.

This does for me, this.

Matty   What?

Jamie   Seeing you.

Matty   Why?

Jamie *doesn't answer. He lets go of* **Matty***'s hand.*

He takes out another sweet. Offers one to **Matty**, *who takes it.
Doesn't open it.* **Jamie** *opens his with real care. Looks at it before he
puts it in his mouth.*

Matty   I keep seeing Ross Mack's cousin. Keeps saying
what he's gonna do to yer. When you get out.

Jamie   Right.

Matty   Shouldn't have fucking done it. Should yer? Should
yer, though, Jamie? Really? Should yer?

Jamie   –

Matty   I never asked you to.

Jamie   No.

Long pause. **Matty** *rubs his eyes with the ball of his fist.*

Jamie   Will you try and find an address for me? Or a phone number or something? Where they've gone. Will yer? Will yer? Will yer, Matty? Please.

Matty   I'll try.

Pause.

Jamie   See this mark. On my finger. Fading now. See that? See my ring? Emma/Lynsey cut into it. Won't let us wear it now. I want a photograph of her. Of Emma. Lynsey won't send us one. I've asked her. Will you get us one?

Matty   I'll try.

Jamie   Will yer? A recent one.

Matty   Yeah.

Long pause.

Jamie   Would've been good, eh? To've watched her . . . y'know.

Matty   Shouldn't have hit Lynsey, then. Shouldn't hit people. Should yer? Should yer, though. Jamie?

Jamie   Don't, Matty.

Just.

Honest.

Jamie *looks away from him.*

Pause.

I don't even dream about outside any more. Not for ages.

Pause.

Matty   If you get a day out, after that, when's your sentence review?

Jamie (*looks back*)   Two years, maybe.

Matty   What'll they say?

Jamie   Don't know. Early to tell. Maybe go to a day-release nick. Just banged up at weekends and night time.

Matty   That'd be good. Wouldn't it? Wouldn't it, though?

Jamie   Yeah. I think so.

Matty   How long we got here?

Jamie   Five minutes. Max. Prob'ly less. Just finish it. When they feel like it sometimes.

Matty   Right.

Pause.

I'm not coping mate.

Pause.

I need you at home.

Pause.

Mum's started talking weird shit. All the time. She's. Dad's no fucking use.

Long pause.

Jamie   If you come again will yer bring us some magazines. Some baccy. Some fucking more teabags. That's good. Do that.

Matty   Yeah. Jamie. I'm sorry about Lynsey. About Emma and that. I don't know what else to say about it.

Jamie   No.

Matty   I should fuck off.

Jamie   Wait.

Matty   Mad this, innit?

Jamie   When they call us. You're not allowed to stand up. All right?

Matty   Right.

Jamie   Mum don't need to come. She's not well. Tell her, tell her, tell her.

Matty   What?

Jamie   Nothing. Just make sure she's. You know.

He leans over and touches **Matt***'s face.* **Matt** *is embarrassed by this. Doesn't know what to do.*

Three

A Saturday afternoon, 15 May 2004, 5.30.

A bedroom in a B & B, Durham Road, Sunderland.

Jamie Carris *is thirty-nine years old.*

There is a big wooden table with two chairs on either side, two blue plates, a teapot, two blue teacups, an opened bottle of milk on it.

A big radio. A notebook and several different coloured pencils.

Window open to outside.

Jamie *wears a blue shirt and jeans.*

He has a cigarette in his hand. Unlit.

Emma Carris *stands at the door. She is seventeen years old. She is wrapped in a big puffa-jacket coat. Her hair is wet, loose, shoulder length.*

Jamie   Your hair's wet.

Emma   I had a shower. Before I came out.

Jamie   Would you like to come in?

Emma   Yeah. Yeah. Yeah. This is . . .

Jamie   What?

Emma   I don't know.

He watches her come into his room.

Jamie   Thank you for coming.

Emma   That's all right.

Jamie   I didn't know. You know. I didn't know what to think or what to say really or anything. It's good. I'm glad. Listen to me. Fucking going on. Sorry.

Emma   No. It's all right. Honest.

Jamie   Would you like a cup of tea?

Emma   Yes I would, please.

Jamie   Sit down. Sit down. Sit down.

He moves a chair back for her to sit on. There are some papers on it.

Emma   Thank you.

Jamie   Move the . . .

Emma   Yeah.

She moves them onto the table. Sits. Doesn't take her coat off.

Jamie   How would you like it?

Emma   Just milk.

Jamie   Right. Milk.

He pours her cup of tea.

Here we are.

He watches her drink it.

Emma   It's nice. Thank you.

Jamie   Would you like a cigarette?

Emma   No, thank you.

Jamie   No, right. Sorry. A sweet?

Emma   A what?

Jamie   Would you like a sweet?

Emma   A sweet? Go on.

She laughs. Takes one. Doesn't open it.

Jamie *opens his. Pops it in his mouth.*

Jamie   You can grow addicted to these. Mess your teeth up something terrible. Taste terrible with tea. Actually. I shouldn't have done that.

Emma   I'll save it.

Jamie   You found the place all right?

Emma   Yeah. It was easy.

Jamie   Was it?

Emma   Durham Road. Easy, that.

Jamie   Right. Good. That's good. You want to take your coat off?

Emma   No. I'm all right.

Jamie   You cold?

Emma   No. I'm fine.

Jamie   Not much, is it?

Emma   What?

Jamie   This place.

Emma   It's all right. I like it.

Jamie   Do yer?

Emma   Bit small. But –

Jamie   Yeah. Owner's all right. Bit weird. Very tall.

Emma   It's good round here.

Jamie   Is it?

Emma   Quite, y'know. Actually it's quite lively. Lot's to do and that.

Jamie   Yeah. Yeah. Yeah. Yeah.

Pause. He stares at her.

Fucking hell, Emma.

Emma   What?

Jamie   Just . . . How old are you now?

Emma   Seventeen.

Jamie   Seventeen. Fucking. I don't believe that, me.

Emma   It's true. Honest.

Jamie   No. I know really. I'm just saying. (*Beat.*) Whereabouts do you live?

Emma   Just up the road. In Tunstall.

Jamie   I've never been to Sunderland before.

Emma   Haven't you?

Jamie   No.

Emma   It's good. I like it.

Jamie   What's Tunstall like?

Emma   It's all right. It's quite nice.

Jamie   I thought it would be raining.

Emma   Did you?

Jamie   That's what you think, innit?

Emma   I don't know.

Jamie   That's what I thought.

Emma   It's not.

Jamie   No. It's all right.

Emma   What should I call you?

Beat. He looks briefly away and then back. Smiles.

Jamie   I don't know.

Emma   What do you think?

Jamie   Jamie. Maybe. Jamie's fine.

Emma   Jamie?

Jamie   Yeah.

Emma   Good. (*Beat.*) After you rang, I wanted to tell you something.

Jamie   Did yer?

Emma   Yeah. That's one of the reasons I came.

Jamie   Is it?

Emma   I'm not sure if I want to any more.

Jamie   Okay.

Emma   I might. We'll wait and see.

Pause, then **Jamie** *leaps to his feet.*

Jamie   Can I show you something.

Emma   What?

Jamie *holds his sovereign ring in her face.*

Jamie   Here. Look at this. This ring. There's an engraving. Can you read that?

Emma   Yeah.

Jamie   I love that. Me.

Emma   It's very big, i'n't it? Shiny and that.

Jamie   Yeah. Yeah. It is. It.

They look at each other for a bit and look away. **Emma** *drinks her tea.*

Emma   I'm shaking. Look at me.

Jamie *doesn't know what to do and so they smile at each other.*

Jamie   You look different.

Emma   Do I?

Jamie   To how I thought you would. You look more.

Emma   What?

Jamie   You look older. You look lovely. Your clothes. Way you dress. (*Beat.*) And you're?

Emma   What?

Jamie   You're working?

Emma   Yeah.

Jamie ~~A, a, a, a?~~

Emma   Receptionist.

Jamie   That's right. In a dentist?

Emma   Yeah.

Jamie   Fucking. That's a good job. That. Isn't it, though? Do you enjoy it?

Emma   I love it, yeah.

Jamie   All them, all them, all them fucking people?

Emma   Yeah.

Jamie   With their teeth.

Emma   I know.

Jamie   That's. Amazing. I hate the dentist, me.

Emma   Why?

Jamie   Scares us.

Emma   Shouldn't. That's stupid.

Jamie   Yeah. Prob'ly. You think you're gonna stay there? At the dentist's?

Emma   Yeah. I think so.

Jamie   That's good.

Emma   They've been saying. Could send us on courses. Send us on a course. Train up. Computer skills. Office management skills. Stick at it. Get the office manager's position.

Jamie   Fucking hell.

Emma   What?

Jamie   Sorry, I shouldn't swear at you.

Emma   It's all right.

Jamie   Office manager. That's incredible to me.

Emma   Why?

Jamie   Just is. Just . . . I'm working.

Emma   Are you?

Jamie   In a garage. In Acton.

Emma   Where's Acton?

Jamie   In the west of London. I love it. You know. Cars. Pick 'em all apart. Look at 'em. Put 'em back together. I like all that. Makes yer think. Gaffer's all right. Bit of a wanker. Not too bad, though. Very quiet.

Emma   How long you been doing that?

Jamie   Since I got out. Six month now.

Emma   Six months?

Jamie   Mad, innit?

Emma   Yeah.

Jamie   So you must have been, at school and that, office manager! You must've been a right boffin.

Emma   A what?

Jamie   Right brainy.

Emma   No. Not really.

Jamie   Must've been, though.

Emma   I wasn't.

Jamie   Where did you go to school?

Emma   Just up our road. Thornhill.

Jamie   Was it all right? Was it?

Emma   Yeah. It was good. It was all right. I liked it. Glad I left.

Jamie   I hated school, me.

Emma   Did you?

Jamie   Wish I could, they should let. Be good to go now. You know what I mean?

Emma   You'd look a bit out of place.

Jamie   Yeah.

Emma   You'd look a bit fucking weird.

Jamie   I was always getting in bother.

Emma   Were yer?

Jamie   With the teachers. Give 'em jip like nothing. Fighting other kids. Kicking off. Tell yer. I was a right little cunt. (*Beat.*) Sorry.

Emma   I wasn't.

Jamie   Thamesview.

Emma   What?

Jamie   That was the name of it. Stupid name. See the river from all over Gravesend. There were Thamesviews fucking all over the place. Nothing special about the school. Fucking. Tell yer.

Emma   Right. This is a bit.

Jamie   I know.

Pause.

Jamie   Are you all right?

Emma   Yeah. I am. I am. I'm. What's it like? Gravesend?

Jamie   It's all right. One whole side of it is the river. There's a big old bridge, up in Dartford which is a bit. I don't really go there much.

Emma   I sometimes think about it.

Jamie   Do you?

Emma   Like to see it, I think. Sometimes.

Jamie   Would yer?

Emma   Don't know.

Pause. She looks at the papers she's moved.

Emma   What you writing?

Jamie   What?

Emma   Your pad. What are you writing?

Jamie   I write the shipping forecast. I listen to it. On the radio. Write it down. Keep a chart. Just keep it recorded. Been doing it years. Started it inside.

Emma   Why?

Jamie   I don't know. Just 'cause. (*Beat.*) You must hate me.

Emma   No. Not hate.

Pause. **Jamie** *stands, moves away from the table. Goes over to the window. Looks out. Runs his hands behind his neck. Then turns to her.*

Jamie   Would you like to go out?

Emma   Out?

Jamie   Go out for a walk or something. We could. Or go and get a coffee. Or something like that.

Emma   No thank you.

Jamie   You could show us what it's like round here.

Emma   I don't think so.

Jamie   If it's good and that. Like you said.

Emma   No.

Jamie   Why not?

Emma   I don't really want to.

Jamie   Right. You want another cup of tea?

Emma   No, thank you.

Jamie   You sure?

Emma   I'll have my sweet now.

Jamie   Good idea.

He watches her unwrap the sweet and start to chew it.

Jamie   How is it?

Emma   It's all right.

Jamie   Good. You sure you're all right in your coat and that?

Emma   I'm fine, yeah.

Jamie   Not hot?

Emma   No. No. No. No.

Jamie *looks at her eating her sweet.*

Jamie   Can I get a photograph of you?

Emma   You what?

Jamie   I don't have any photographs of you. Since you were a baby.

Emma   Right.

Jamie   I wanted to write to you. But that was a bit −

Emma   I don't know what photographs I've got. I don't really keep any photographs.

Jamie   No?

Emma   I can ask Mum.

Jamie   Yeah. That'd be. I'd like that. How is she? Your Mum?

Emma   She's all right. She's well. Dad and that.

Jamie   I came to try and find you once.

Emma   Did yer?

Jamie   I had a day release. Tried to come up to Manchester. Didn't go too well.

Emma   No?

Jamie   No. Matty got your address for us and everything.

Emma   I remember Uncle Matty.

Jamie   Yeah?

Emma   I used to like him, I think. I think I used to think he was quite funny.

Jamie   Yeah. He still is.

Emma   What's he doing?

Jamie   He's married. He's, he's, he's thirty. Does a bit of chippying. Down Gravesend still. He's doing all right, y'know?

Emma   Yeah.

Jamie   I think it's great you're going to get more, do more training, get all that stuff. I think that's important. That makes me very proud of you.

Emma   Why?

Jamie   It just does. It's good to know things like that.

Emma   Right. I see.

Jamie   Should hear how you speak. Honestly. It's like.

Emma   What?

Jamie   Nothing. Look at you.

Emma   What?

Jamie   Your fucking, your hair and that!

Emma   What about it?

Jamie   It don't matter.

Beat.

Emma   Can I have a drink of water, please?

Jamie   Yeah. Yes. Yes. Yes. Of course you can.

He fetches her a glass of water. He can't watch her drink it.

Emma   You know one thing I remember about you?

Jamie   What?

Emma   I might have got this wrong.

Jamie   What?

Emma   When I was little, did I find a wasps' nest?

Jamie   Fucking hell.

Emma   I was tiny.

Jamie   That's right.

Emma   I remember that. I remember finding this thing, this, this, nest. Getting a big stick, I remember, and all these wasps come out of it. All I remember. I'm screaming. They're going in my mouth. And you come. And pick me up. And run with me. Is that right? Did this happen? Going to hospital with you. Both of us. Our skin all stung.

Jamie   You were about three.

Emma   I remember that.

Jamie   Emma.

Emma   What?

Jamie   –

Emma   What?

Jamie   I think it's good that you remember some things.

Emma   I don't remember much.

Jamie   No.

He pulls a cigarette from the packet in his shirt pocket.

Do you mind if I smoke this?

Emma   No.

Jamie   Are you sure?

Emma Yeah.

Jamie Should I open the window?

Emma Yeah.

Jamie *does. Then turns and looks at her for a while.*

Jamie Do you remember going to the park with us?

Emma I'm not sure.

Jamie I used to take you. Take you down the river. There's a park there. Little lake. Go on the swings and that. Give you a bit of a push. Play. Take you to the library sometimes. Get a book for you to look at. Looking at all the pictures and that. Take you on the ferry sometimes. We used to do that. Do you remember?

Emma I don't think so.

Jamie We did. I did. I used to do that. Did your mum not say?

Emma No.

Jamie Did she never tell you?

Emma No. She didn't.

Jamie When she took you up to Essex. You were, you must have been, I think, three. Maybe. She took you up there. I used to come and see you. Weekends. Go over the river. You used to come and meet us off the ferry sometimes. That was where the wasps' nest was. A field. Just behind your new flat. I remember all that.

Emma I just remember feeling them in my mouth. It was frightening.

Jamie You must remember more than that, though.

Emma I don't.

Jamie You must, though, love.

Emma I really don't. Honestly.

Jamie *clenches his fist and holds it behind his head.*

Jamie When you was born. You was, like. You was a breach. Is the word. And they had to do an operation. I remember thinking what if anything happened to your mum. And when you was a baby. The way your skin felt. I've never felt anything. Your eyes. And all your, all your, your hair.

Emma Jamie.

Jamie Yeah?

No response.

What?

Emma You're starting to scare me a bit.

Jamie To *scare* you?

Emma Just a bit. Don't panic.

Jamie Right. I'm –

Emma I shouldn't be here, y'know?

Jamie Why shouldn't you?

Emma I never told Mum. I think she'd be a bit upset.

Jamie She'd be fine.

Emma I don't want to be too late.

Jamie No. (*Beat.*) I remember the smell of you.

Emma –

Jamie And how I could, when you were crying, how I knew it was you.

Emma Please don't do this.

Jamie Do what?

Emma I should probably go.

Jamie Emma.

Emma   I did really want to see you, Jamie. I just wasn't expecting you to ring me up.

Jamie   I know.

Emma   I don't even know who you are or anything. And now I think −

Jamie   Emma.

Emma   I shouldn't have come. I was probably just being stupid. I don't know what you want me to do, or . . .

Jamie   I wanted to.

Emma   What?

Jamie   I wanted to see you.

Emma   Yeah, well, you've seen me now.

Jamie   Your gran's died.

Emma   I never knew her.

Jamie   Nearly ten years back. I was inside. They let us go out for the funeral.

Emma   I never knew her.

Jamie   When you were little my thing for you was I always wanted you to be better than her.

Emma   I never knew her. You might as well be talking Chinese to me.

Jamie   Don't say that.

Emma   You might.

Jamie   You remember coming to see us, in the nick?

Emma   No.

Jamie   You must do.

Emma   I don't, all right.

Jamie   The officers checked your socks. Made you take your socks off to look for, for, to look for.

Emma   I don't remember.

Jamie   Are you lying?   *I slap you*

Emma   What?

Jamie   Are you?   *I push you*

Emma   No!

Jamie   You must be.   *I examine you*

Emma   I'm going.

Jamie   Don't.

Emma   Shouldn't call people liars. I am. I'm leaving.

Jamie   Don't. Emma. Please. (*Beat.*) Please.

Emma *stops. Looks at him for some time. Bites her thumb. Looks away. Goes to the window. Looks out.*

Emma   You know when you rang us. I had something I wanted to tell you. Do you know what it was?

Jamie   No.

Emma   Were you on *Crimewatch*?

Jamie   You what?

Emma   Were you? Mum told us. Said she went nuts. I'd throttle yer.

Jamie   Yeah.

Pause. **Emma** *smiles at him. Looks out of the window. And then back.*

Emma   You're not my dad. That was what I wanted to tell you. Not any more.

Pause.

I've got a dad. It's not you.

Pause.

I lied about you all the time. Until I was about. Ten. Maybe older. Then I stopped lying.

Pause.

Can I ask you a question?

Jamie   Course.

Emma   You killed somebody. Didn't yer?

Jamie   What?

Emma   Who was it?

Jamie   It was a man called Ross Mack.

Emma   Why did you do it?

Pause.

Jamie *looks at her, doesn't flinch.*

He rubs his hand over the back of his head.

Jamie   It doesn't matter.

Emma   Why, though?

Jamie   It doesn't matter, really.

Emma   What was it like?

Jamie   Don't.

Emma   What was it? Jamie? What was it like?

Jamie   I don't talk about this.

Emma   If you tell us, I'll stay.

Jamie   I wish I could go back in time. Turn my body back in time. Screw myself up into a, I don't know, a knot and go back and not do it. I have tried.

Emma *looks at him for a while.*

Emma   What was it like inside?

Jamie   I can't do this.

Emma   You've got to. If I've got to, you've got to. That's fair.

Jamie *looks back at her before he speaks. Raises his hand as if to touch her, even from a distance away. Can't. Lowers it again. Turns away.*

Jamie   When I left Wandsworth. Which was the last place I was at. Before I went to Latchmere House. There was a photograph, on the wall of the gate, of a prisoner who'd just been released. He was hanging around. Outside the nick. Following the screws. He couldn't leave it. Couldn't cope without it. (*Beat.*) Screws say to yer, when yer going, 'See yer soon.' (*Beat.*) When I come out. Just stood there. Couldn't move. Couldn't move my legs.

Pause.

I was so tired. On the way up here. Like when yer bones get tired.

Pause.

I want you to forgive me for the things that I've done.

Emma   To forgive you?

Jamie   I want you to forgive me for the things that I've done.

Pause.

I want you to forgive me for the things that I've done.

Emma   I know.

Jamie   I want you to.

Emma   I know.

Jamie   I want you to.

Emma   I don't know if I can.

Jamie   I never wanted to be separated from you. Not ever.

Emma   I know.

Jamie   I've wanted to see you every day. All the time.

Emma   That isn't my fault.

Jamie   I wanted so many things for you.

Emma   That doesn't mean anything.

Jamie   It does to me.

Emma   But it doesn't. Not really.

Jamie   As I get older. All I want now is things for you. For you to be safe. For you to have money and to be safe. And all the things that you want. For you to get them. Tell me one thing.

Emma   What?

Jamie   Tell me one thing that you want.

Emma   I can't think.

Jamie   Please tell me.

Emma   I'd like to fly a plane.

Jamie   I think that's brilliant, that. That stops me breathing.

Pause. He goes to the window.

Fucking. It's cold. Isn't it?

Emma   Yeah.

Jamie   I should close the window.

He stands still for a bit. Then closes the window.

Very long pause. The two stand absolutely still.

Emma   Can I go?

Jamie   What?

Emma   I want to go now.

Jamie   Right.

He doesn't look back at her.

Emma   Mum'll be wondering where I've got to.

Jamie   Right.

Emma   I'm not going to tell her.

Jamie   Right. I loved her more than I loved you. And that's . . .

A slight pause.

Sometimes I go out without a light for my cigarettes on purpose just so that I can ask somebody for a light. So that I can talk to them.

A longer pause.

Emma   When are you going home, Jamie?

Jamie   Tomorrow.

Emma   Right. Back to Acton?

Jamie   Yeah. (*Beat. Looking away from her.*) I want to hold your soul. In my hands. Cup it.

Emma   I don't know what that means.

Jamie   Would you like to see me again, one day? Would you like that, do you think?

Emma   I don't know.

Jamie   You could come down to Gravesend if you wanted to. One time. Doesn't need to be for a while.

Emma   I don't know.

Jamie   Have you ever been to Margate? I could take you to Margate. Would you like to go to Margate?

Emma   No. Maybe yeah. Probably not.

Pause.

They stand still for a while yet.

I should be going.

Jamie   I know. Yeah. I'm sorry.

Emma   Do I just close the door to behind me?

Jamie   What?

Emma   The latch, do I just pull it to behind me?

Jamie   Yeah. You do. That's. I won't come down with you.

Emma   No. I'm glad I've seen you.

Jamie *pulls a scrap of card from his pocket and a pen and writes a phone number.*

Jamie   Here. This is the number of the garage where I work. Will you ring us one day? When you're ready to?

Emma *takes the number.*

Long pause.

She goes to the door.

Emma   Thank you. I'll. Yeah. I'll. Bye, Jamie.

Jamie   Bye, love.

Emma *leaves.*

Jamie *sits at the table. Goes to kick it over. Can't.*

Stares at it.

Four

Thursday 13 July 1983, 5.30 p.m.

Windmill Hill, Gravesend, Kent. A beautiful sunny day. Hot bright sky. There are the sounds of distant cars, birds.

Jamie Carris *is eighteen. He is wearing work-clothes.* **Lynsey Sergeant** *is fifteen. She is wearing a school uniform. But only shirt, skirt, tie. Shirt sleeves rolled up. Shirt hanging out. Hair tied back off her face.*

They lie on their backs, looking up at the clouds. He props his hand on his elbow, playing with his chest.

There is some time before they talk to one another.

Jamie *starts to chuckle. Gets quite loud.*

Lynsey   Ssshhhh.

Jamie   What?

Lynsey   You. Calm down. It's all right now. It's quiet here. It's good.

Pause.

She touches his arm, strokes it slightly, then points her hand up to one of the clouds.

That one looks like an old man's face.

Jamie   Where?

Lynsey   There.

Jamie   Oh yeah. With a beard.

Lynsey   Ha!

Jamie   Jimmy Hill.

Pause.

I don't want to go work. Not now.

Lynsey   Don't then.

Jamie   I so don't want to.

Pause.

Jamie   How long you got?

Lynsey   Not long. They'll start looking for us prob'ly. Are you sure you're all right?

Jamie   Yeah. Course. I'm glad you're here. Thank you for coming.

Lynsey   'S all right. Psycho.

Pause.

Jamie   She's a stupid cow. She's fucking mental. Just looks at us. I walked out.

Lynsey   What was he doing?

Jamie   She's sat on top of him. Skirt hitched up her arse. Fat cunt. Eyes rolling back in his head. Gary Noolan, for fuck's sake! I should go back and find him.

Lynsey   Fuck off.

Jamie   He'll be in the Station Arms. Bet yer. Should go and glass the cunt.

Lynsey   Don't, Jamie. Serious.

Long pause.

Jamie   I'm thirsty.

Lynsey   I'm hot.

Jamie   Yeah

Slight pause. **Lynsey** *rolls over on her stomach to look at him.* **Jamie** *doesn't look at her.*

Lynsey   Should take our tops off.

Jamie   Yeah.

Lynsey   Should do. No one'd see.

Jamie   Psycho.

Lynsey   Chicken.

Chicken impersonations. **Jamie** *chuckles.*

Jamie (*cod hard guy*)   Shut it.

Long pause.

Jamie   I like you. (*Beat.*) You make us laugh.

Lynsey   Listen to you!

Jamie   What?

Lynsey (*imitating him*)   'I like you. You make us laugh.'

She picks at the ground.

You think Matty's dad knows? About your mum and Noolan?

Jamie   Don't know.

Lynsey   What's he like, Matty's dad?

Jamie   Al? He's all right. Quiet. Don't mind him. Just sits there most of the time.

He snorts a half laugh.

Long pause.

How is school?

Lynsey (*suppressed laugh*)   Terrible.

They burst out laughing.

You know Mr Mackenzie?

Jamie   Yeah.

Lynsey   I bit him.

Jamie   You what?

Lynsey   Bit his hand. Bleeding and everything.

Jamie   You're fucking crackers, you.

Lynsey   I'm in Art, yeah? And Jones goes 'Get out.' Sends us out. I ain't even done nothing. So I won't go. Start throwing things around. Paint and that.

Jamie   Why?

Lynsey   Just 'cause. He goes and gets Mackenzie and he grabs us round the waist. So I just bit him. Did his head.

Jamie   I bet.

Lynsey   Fucking going red. 'You BIT me!! You BIT me!!'

Jamie   Reckon he'll suspend you?

Lynsey   No. Hope so.

Long pause.

Jamie   How's Clarence House?

Lynsey   Same. You're better off at home.

Jamie   I'm gonna get you out.

Lynsey   Are yer?

Jamie   Yeah. Go back and get yer. Do a break out. Come and stay at ours.

Lynsey   You reckon?

Jamie   I am. (*Beat.*) Be better if you were there. She wouldn't do my head in so much.

Long pause.

Then **Lynsey** *starts laughing.*

Lynsey   Guess what I'm thinking about.

Jamie   No.

Lynsey   Go on.

Jamie   No.

Lynsey   (*drawling the name out like a child*)   Jamie.

Jamie   No.

Lynsey   Remember when I found yer?

Jamie   Yeah.

Lynsey   Fucking hanging there.

She carries on laughing. He doesn't laugh.

Lynsey   Got to admit it's quite funny.

Jamie   Idiot.

Lynsey   It is though. I'n't it? I'n't it funny? Spoilsport.

Pause.

You got any bruises?

Jamie   Yeah.

Lynsey   Still?

Jamie   Yeah.

Lynsey   Show us.

Jamie *pulls down his collar to reveal his neck.*

Lynsey   You looked mad.

Jamie (*smiling*)   Fuck off.

Lynsey   You seen mine?

Jamie   No.

Lynsey (*points to her thigh*)   Here?

Jamie   No.

Lynsey *pulls up her skirt to reveal the skin on her thigh.*

Lynsey   You really never seen this?

Jamie   No. How d'you get that?

Lynsey   When I was little I was climbing a tree. Fell. Got a branch through my leg. You wanna touch it? You can touch it.

Jamie *does.*

Don't feel nothing.

Jamie   It's rough. The skin.

Lynsey   Yeah.

Jamie *strokes it for a while. Then bends down and kisses the scar.*

Lynsey *smiles.*

He leans over, slightly clumsily, and kisses her lips.

She smiles.

He moves away from her.

She leans back on her elbows. Smiles at him.

Lynsey   That was nice. Don't need to stop, yer know?

Jamie *breaks away. Stands up.*

Lynsey *looks at him, trying to get inside his head.*

He looks down at her.

She smiles. He looks away.

Pause.

Lynsey   I should probably go.

Jamie *(turns to look at her)*   Don't.

Lynsey   I don't want to. I've got to. You know what they're like. They do their nut if I'm gone too long.

Jamie *looks away.*

Jamie   You wanna go for a drive later?

Lynsey   Maybe.

Jamie   Should I come round?

Lynsey   Yeah.

Jamie *(looks back)*   After I've been to the Station Arms? Found Gary Noolan?

Lynsey   Don't.

Jamie   I'm going to.

Lynsey   Jamie. I'm warning you.

Jamie   Are you?

Lynsey   Yeah.

Jamie (*he looks right at her*)   Stay with us, then.

Lynsey   I can't.

Jamie   You can.

Lynsey   I want to get back.

Jamie   *Do* yer?

Slight pause.

Lynsey *can't reply.*

Jamie *looks away.*

Jamie   Al reckoned we was gonna go Margate.

Lynsey   When?

Jamie   All of us. Soon. You should come with us.

Lynsey   Yeah. Maybe. All right.

Jamie *looks up, right high up at the moon.* **Lynsey** *watches him. Laughs. Lies back down.*

He puts his hands on his hips and smiles down at her.

Slow fade on the lights to black.

Lightning Source UK Ltd.
Milton Keynes UK
UKOW040955010812

196884UK00005B/5/P